Salt Lick Productions in association with Omnibus Theatre
present

SLIPPERY

by Louis Emmitt-Stern

Slippery was first performed at the Omnibus Theatre, London, on 17 March 2026,
directed by Matthew Iliffe.

SLIPPERY

by Louis Emmitt-Stern

Cast in order of speaking

Kyle	**Perry Williams**
Jude	**John McCrea**

Writer	**Louis Emmitt-Stern**
Director	**Matthew Iliffe**
Set and Costume Designer	**Hannah Schmidt**
Lighting Designer	**Ryan Joseph Stafford**
Sound Designer	**Anna Short**
Casting Director	**Nadine Rennie CDG**
Intimacy Director	**Jess Tucker Boyd**
Dramaturg	**Gillian Greer**
Production Manager	**Thomas J. Quine**
Stage Manager	**Ann Bailey**
Associate Producer	**Lucy Jessica**

Approximate running time 85 minutes

Cast

Perry Williams – Kyle

Credits include: Player Kings (Noël Coward Theatre, West End); Little Women (UK Tour) and Maud (The Vaults).

Film: Ghostbusters: Frozen Empire for Sony Pictures.

Training: Perry Williams trained at the Royal Academy of Dramatic Art.

John McCrea – Jude

Credits include: Prince F*ggot (Playwrights Horizons/Seaview Productions); Cabaret (Playhouse Theatre – KitKat Club); "Daddy": A Melodrama (Almeida Theatre); Everybody's Talking About Jamie (Apollo Theatre/Sheffield Theatres).

Film: Think of England; Femme; Cruella; She Will; Everybody's Talking About Jamie; God's Own Country.

Television: Father Brown; We Hunt Together; Pistol; Giri/Haji; Dracula.

Awards: Laurence Olivier Award nomination for Everybody's Talking About Jamie.

Creatives

Writer – Louis Emmitt-Stern

Credits include: I F*cked You in My Spaceship (Soho Theatre & VAULT Festival); Mansfield Park adapted from the novel by Jane Austen (Jane Austen's House & Guildford School of Acting); Snakes and Ladders (Southwark Playhouse/Oxford School of Drama).

Training: Royal Central School of Speech and Drama (MFA); Soho Theatre Writers Lab and Alumni Group; National Theatre Young Playwrights Programme; Lyric Hammersmith Young Directors Course; and Oxford Playhouse Playmakers.

Awards: Soho Theatre's Tony Craze Award; VAULT Festival Origins Award for Outstanding New Work.

Director – Matthew Iliffe

Credits include: SKYE (Summerhall, Edinburgh Fringe); Foam (Finborough Theatre); Bacon (Finborough Theatre, touring, SoHo Playhouse, NYC and Korea); Four Play (Above The Stag); The Burnt Part Boys (Park Theatre).

As assistant or associate: Starter For Ten (Bristol Old Vic/Birmingham Rep); Assassins (Chichester Festival Theatre).

Training: Matthew trained on the National Theatre Directors Course and holds a BA in Theatre & Performance Studies from the University of Bristol.

Awards: Best Direction Off-West End Award; Best Production at LPT's Standing Ovation Awards (twice).

Matthew is currently a Dramaturg for the Women's Prize for Playwriting.

Set and Costume Designer – Hannah Schmidt

Credits include: Dracula (National Youth Theatre); The Passenger (Finborough Theatre); Personal Values (Hampstead Theatre); The Idiot (Royal Central School of Speech and Drama); Whole (South-East England tour); Hansel and Gretel (The Big House).

As assistant or associate: Kyoto (The Lincoln Centre New York); The Land of the Living (National Theatre); Rhino (Almeida Theatre); Fear of 13 (Donmar

Warehouse); A Moon for the Misbegotten (Almeida Theatre); Michael Kohlhaas (Schaubühne am Lehniner Platz); Die Gute Erde (Staatstheater Kassel).

Awards: Best Designer Stage Debut Award; Best Set Design BroadwayWorldUK Awards (nomination).

Lighting Designer – Ryan Joseph Stafford

Credits include: Our Town (Welsh National Theatre, Rose Theatre Kingston); More Life (Royal Court); The Exhibition (The Royal Ballet, London); Kontakthof: Echoes of '78 (Tanztheater Wuppertal, Sadler's Wells, Theatertreffen, Berlin); Hot Mess (Birmingham Hippodrome, Edinburgh Fringe 2025, Southwark Playhouse, Fringe First Award); Scenes from the Climate Era (Gate Theatre); KABEL (Sadler's Wells East); KISMET: Gallery of Consequence (Rambert); Olion (Frân Wen); Rope (Theatr Clwyd); Natalia Osipova: Force of Nature (New York City Center, International Tour); Bacon (Finborough, touring, SoHo Playhouse NYC and Korea); Vortex (Russell Maliphant Dance Company); Can This Place Be A Temple? (The Place, UK Tour); Grimeboy (Birmingham Rep); Dance for Ukraine (London Coliseum); Codi (National Dance Company of Wales); Isla (Theatr Clwyd & Royal Court); Generation Goldfish (Bayerisches Staatsballett, Munich); Left from Write (Norwegian National Ballet); To Start With (Sadler's Wells); Shades of Blue (Sadler's Wells); Together, Not the Same (Sadler's Wells).

Training: Ryan trained at Rose Bruford College, graduating with a First Class BA Honours Degree in Lighting Design. Ryan received a Masters with Distinction in Art & Politics from Goldsmiths, University of London, following his research into 'Political Light'.

Awards: Best Lighting Design Off-West End Award; Association of Lighting Designers' Michael Northern Award for Excellence in Lighting Design.

Sound Designer – Anna Short

Credits include: And Then Come the Nightjars (Theatre Royal Bury St Edmunds); Lark Rise to Candleford (Watermill Theatre); The Girls Bathroom: Live (Hammersmith Apollo); Jurassic (Soho Theatre); Count Dykula (Soho Theatre); Even More... Ghost Stories by Candlelight (UK Tour); Get Happy (Omnibus Theatre – Fringe Theatre Award Nomination for Sound Design and Production); The Maladies (Kiln Theatre); Canned Goods (Southwark Playhouse); Nunsense (English Theatre Frankfurt); Beyond Her Years (Almeida Theatre); Lady Dealer (Roundabout, Summerhall & Bush Theatre).

As associate: Folk (Hampstead Theatre); My Son's a Queer (But What Can You Do?) (Turbine Theatre).

Casting Director – Nadine Rennie CDG

Credits include: Ukraine Unbroken (Arcola); The Pitchfork Disney (Kings Head Theatre); ELMET (Javaad Alipoor Company); LIFERS (Southwark Playhouse); 2024 Papatango New Writing Prize winner The Meat Kings! (Inc) of Brooklyn Heights (Park Theatre); Providers (Synergy Theatre at Brixton House); Expendable (Royal Court); Miracle on 34th Street (HOME Manchester); Pig Heart Boy (Unicorn/tour); Wish You Were Here (Gate); The Flea (Yard); My Mother's Funeral: The Show (Paines Plough); Miss Julie (Park); Dead Girls Rising (Silent Uproar); We Could All Be Perfect (Sheffield Theatres); He Said She Said (Kiln); Wreckage (King's Head); Breeding (King's Head); Leaves of Glass (Park); Further Than The Furthest Thing (Minack); SHED: Exploded View (Royal Exchange); Bacon (Finborough/touring/Soho Playhouse NYC); Es & Flo (WMC & Kiln); Super High Resolution (Soho); Britannicus (Lyric); The Breach (Hampstead); The Ministry of Lesbian Affairs (Soho); Typical Girls (Sheffield Theatres); Run Sister Run (Paines Plough); Little Baby Jesus (Orange Tree); The Last King of Scotland (Sheffield Theatres); There Are No Beginnings (Leeds).

Nadine is a Creative Associate at Synergy Theatre Project. Prior to going freelance, Nadine was in-house Casting Director at Soho Theatre for over fifteen years.

Intimacy Director – Jess Tucker Boyd

Credits include: The Tattooist of Auschwitz (Sky/Peacock); One Day (Netflix); The Winter King (Bad Wolf Productions); I Hate Suzie (Sky); Both Sides Now (Sky Studios); Buckingham Murders (TBM Productions); Foam (Finborough Theatre); Bacon (Finborough/touring/Soho Playhouse NYC); Faustus: That Damned Woman (Lyric Hammersmith); Missing Julie (Theatre Clwyd).

Movement direction includes: Hakawatis: Women of the Arabian Nights (Shakespeare's Globe); Katzenmusik (Royal Court Theatre); My English

Persian Kitchen (Soho Theatre); BU21 (Theatre 503/ Trafalgar Studios); Bottom (Bristol Old Vic).

Training: She trained through Ita O'Brien (Intimacy On Set) and holds an MA in Movement Directing & Teaching (Distinction) from Royal Central School of Speech and Drama.

Jess is Movement Lead for BA Acting for Stage and Screen at University of West London. Her play A Deprivation Just & Wise was longlisted for RSC 37 Plays and is in development for film under mentorship from the Royal Court Theatre.

Dramaturg – Gillian Greer

Dramaturgy includes: The Secret Garden (Regent's Park Open Air Theatre); Kathy & Stella Solve a Murder! (Edinburgh Fringe, touring and Ambassadors Theatre, West End).

Plays include: Boy Parts, adapted from the novel by Eliza Clark (Soho Theatre); Petals (Theatre Upstairs, Dublin); Meat (Theatre503); Near FM (Radio).

Awards: Celtic Media Festival Award (Best Radio Drama); Irish Times Theatre Award for Best New Play (nomination); Theatre503 International Playwriting Award (shortlisted).

Gillian is currently Associate Dramaturg at the Royal Court, after being Literary Manager at Soho Theatre. She is currently developing new work with Abbey Theatre, Ireland and 45 North Productions, London.

Production Manager – Thomas J. Quine

Credits include: Anne of Green Gables, NEZHA (Emma Wang Productions Ltd.); Before the Millenium (Old Fire Station Oxford); Sense & Sensibility, Theo In-Between (British Youth Music Theatre); Tuck Everlasting (National Youth Music Theatre); The Jungle Book (Wiltshire Creative); Unfiltered (Pentabus); NOSTOS, The Gel, Table, Callisto and Snakes and Ladders (all Oxford School of Drama); Even More Ghost Stories by Candlelight (UK Tour) MAKE ME- Workshop (HighTide) L'Incoronazione di Poppea and La Cenerentola (both Hampstead Garden Opera); On|Off Presents The Disruptors (London Fashion Week 2025); Homo Alone (The Other Palace); Dahling you were Marvellous, Lemons Lemons Lemons Lemons Lemons, Pool (no water), Afterlife (all RCSSD); Shrek, Loserville, Carrie (all University of Chichester); DogShit (Theatre 503).

As assistant / associate: The Code (Deus Ex Machina); Macbeth (Dukes Theatre Company); Cavalleria Rusticana (Blackheath Halls); Into the Woods and Spring Awakening (both Royal Academy of Music); The Dream of a Ridiculous Man and The Dry House (both Marylebone Theatre).

Stage Manager – Ann Bailey

Credits include: Marina Abramović: Balkan Erotic Epic (Aviva Studios); The Burnt City (Punchdrunk); How to Survive an Apocalypse (Finborough Theatre) and Hitchhiker's Guide to the Galaxy Immersive (Riverside Studios).

Ann holds an MA in Stage and Event Management from Royal Welsh College of Music and Drama and specialises in Immersive and fringe theatre.

Associate Producer – Lucy Jessica

Lucy is a London based producer working across television, film and theatre. Recent credits include: Living Memory: 2006 (Series, Lip Mouth Studios) and Uncle Artoo (Short, Macaw Media).

As Line or Assistant Producer credits include: The Country (Shy Billy Productions), Amigos (Short, Excellent Question); Ain't Nuff Time (Imagine If).

Lucy's extensive experience as a Production Assistant and 2nd AD includes work on music videos for artists such as Central Cee and Blanco, as well as a series for Channel 4.0 and branded content for Amazon, GRAFT3R, and SDMN. She continues to develop an ambitious and evolving slate of projects and is always seeking out bold, original stories.

OMNIBUS THEATRE

Omnibus Theatre is a multi-award-winning independent theatre in Clapham, South London. Finalist in the Fringe Theatre of the Year 2020 and 2023 The Stage Awards, Off-West End Award winner 2018 and 2020, and recipient of the Peter Brook/Royal Court Theatre Support Award in 2016. The heart of the organisation's ambitious programme lies in classics re-imagined, modern revivals and new writing. Omnibus Theatre also provides a platform for LGBTQ+ work and aims to give voice to the underrepresented and challenge perceptions.

LONDON FRIEND **Charity Partner**

Established in 1972 London Friend is the UK's oldest Lesbian, Gay, Bisexual and Trans charity. They support the health and mental wellbeing of the LGBT community in and around London, offering counselling and support around issues such as same-sex relationships, sexual and gender identity and promoting personal growth and self-confidence.

London Friend is also home to Antidote – the UK's oldest LGBT drug and alcohol service, offering social groups which provide a safe space to meet and socialise as an alternative to the bar and club scene.

SLIPPERY

Acknowledgements

I wrote the first draft of *Slippery* on Soho Theatre's Writers' Lab. It would be cliché to say it changed my life, but it wouldn't be untrue. Thank you to everyone who supported me during my attachment, for giving me a creative home, championing my work, and believing in this play. Lakesha Arie-Angelo, Chris White, David Luff, Ameena Hamid, Jessy Roberts and Adam Brace. An extended thank you to Jules Haworth, who, through kindness and encouragement, has quietly raised a generation of British playwrights, not least of all this one.

John Fitzpatrick, Nathan Ellis, Joseph Winer, Tom Wright, Jennifer Farmer and Paris Hoxton, for reading and rereading this play, all at different stages but with equal insight and generosity.

Lucy Jane Atkinson, for nurturing the earliest versions of this play with such detail and care.

The Kyles and Judes over the many years of development: Benedict Salter and Leo Wan, Lee Knight and Dominic Holmes, William Robinson and Pedro Leandro.

Marie McCarthy, Sam Pout and the team at Omnibus Theatre for picking us up and giving this play a home.

Matthew Iliffe, for being my running mate and getting the play over the line when it looked like it might live its life in a drawer. Thanks for your friendship, your leadership, and our rigorous dramaturgical discussions on the carbonara recipe. You've made this play undeniably tastier.

The delicious team who have brought this play to life: John McCrea and Perry Williams. Hannah Schmidt, Ryan Joseph Stafford, Anna Short, Jess Tucker Boyd, Nadine Rennie, Lucy Jessica, Thomas Quinn and Ann Bailey.

Dan, Poppy, Pat, and all at London Friend.

Maddie Hindes, Matt Applewhite, Deborah Halsey, Beth Archer, and all at Nick Hern Books.

Maddie O'Dwyer, for reading this play, taking me to the pub and offering to represent me when all I could offer in return was a pint and a pipe dream.

Chloe, Harry, Wilco. Adam. Mum and Dad. I couldn't do it without you.

Finally, Gill Greer, without whom this play would not exist, and neither would this writer. Thank you.

L.E-S.
2026

'We're not who we used to be
We're just two ghosts standing in the place of you and me
Trying to remember how it feels to have a heartbeat'

Harry Styles, 'Two Ghosts'

Characters

KYLE
JUDE

Both are a similar age

Setting

Action takes place in a real room, in real time.

Note on Text

(/) indicates the point of interruption in overlapping dialogue.

(…) indicates trailing off.

(–) indicates interruption. Within speech it indicates a break in syntax.

(,) on a separate line indicates deliberate silence from pressure, expectation or desire to speak.

Words in [square brackets] are unspoken, indicating an unfinished thought.

Punctuation is used freely and artistically to suggest delivery, not to conform to grammatical rules.

This text went to press before the end of rehearsals and so may differ slightly from the play as performed.

Three a.m. A half-furnished kitchen-living-dining room in a state-of-the-art penthouse apartment. Canary Wharf. London. Incomplete but tidy. It's immaculate, and totally impersonal.

KYLE *isn't sure where to stand.* JUDE *is off in the bathroom.*

KYLE Looks fine.
Honestly.

JUDE (*Off.*) It's awful.
I look fucking awful.

KYLE It's not even that bad.
Not like you've been attacked

JUDE (*Off.*) Attacked?

KYLE Like really fucking gashed, or

JUDE (*Off.*) Jesus.

KYLE You just slipped, didn't you?
A bad fall.

,

Wasn't it?

,

Don't you have another mirror?

JUDE (*Off.*) Two seconds

KYLE Bedroom mirror?

JUDE (*Off.*) Looking in the light.

KYLE Just I'm
Fucking
Bursting
A little bit.

So
Whenever you're done

...

No pressure

KYLE*'s phone rings. He looks. Doesn't answer.*

JUDE (*Off.*) Makes me look fat.

KYLE What's that?

JUDE My face.
Do you think it makes my face look fat?

KYLE You look great.

JUDE (*Off.*) Makes me look puffy, a bit.

KYLE You look perfect.
You look spectacular.
Why would you look puffy?

JUDE (*Off.*) Just do, just –
Spectacular?

KYLE Well...
not *Spectacular*
No.
Not...

JUDE (*Off.*) Is this you being funny or...?

KYLE What should I say?
What do you want me to say, Jude?
Should I say: 'yes, it's awful, quite frankly it's fucking awful, all those years of skincare, all the L'Oréal and Clinique, might as well have not bothered, might as well have saved the money because you've fucked it for yourself now, and if you're even thinking about leaving the house without a paper bag over your head, you've got a whole lot more confidence than me, babe.'

,

How's that?

,

Is that what I should say?

JUDE (*Off.*) That's what you should never
ever /
EVER
say.

KYLE No, I know
No of course I'm not –

JUDE (*Off.*) *Ever.*

KYLE It was hyperbole.
Was being ironic.

Think it's quite attractive, actually.

JUNE (*Off.*) Stop.

KYLE That 'rough and ready' sort of look.

JUDE (*Off.*) Stop talking.

KYLE Looks
Kind of… foxy.

JUDE (*Off.*) *Foxy?*

KYLE Like 'Rwaawrrr' like
Foxy
You know

JUDE (*Off.*) Right.

KYLE It's a compliment

JUDE (*Off.*) Is it?

KYLE People say that.

It's a thing
It's a thing people say.
It's a word.

His phone buzzes.

A message.

He glances down.

Then puts the phone away.

And fuck it anyway. What people think. What anyone thinks.
Personally think it's cool.
It's a story, isn't it? It's a little story, like…
People will say
'Oh, how did that happen'
and it's quite cool, to to to have that. That story.
That conversation-starter.
You know
A cheeky little conversation-starter
That's…
Yeah, what I think.

,

Doesn't matter.
Doesn't even matter what I think
So

Silence.

You okay?

Nothing.

He waits.

Starts to shift around a little.

It slowly becomes a dance.

The 'I need a pee' dance.

(*Singing.*) I am going to wee myself
wee wee wee my pants
oh, my pants, oh gonna be so soggy and cold
fuck me

Stops moving.

Takes a deep breath.

One Mississippi
Two Mississippi
Three Mississippi
Four Mississippi
Five Mis…

He clocks a vase on a shelf.

He's thinking about it.

He can't… can he?

…Mississippi

Walks over.

Looks a little closer.

Looks back.

Nothing.

A moment.

He unzips.

Takes the vase.

Another moment.

As he positions it, he spots something inside.

Reaches in and pulls out a gram of methamphetamine in a baggie.

A longer moment.

He's not that desperate any more.

JUDE (*Off.*) Kettle on?

…

Kyle?

KYLE Yeah?

JUDE (*Off.*) Can you put the kettle on.

KYLE I'll do it, I'm doing it.

He puts the baggie back in the vase. Puts the vase back on the shelf.

Before he can get to the kettle…

JUDE *is out. He's in suit trousers and white work shirt covered in blood. A gash on his forehead has been stitched up and dressed. Another on his left forearm, also dressed. His sleeve rolled up to accommodate. His hair is fucking perfect.*

Been holding it since we left.

He rushes into the bathroom.

JUDE *fills the kettle from the tap.*

JUDE Didn't fancy going there?

KYLE (*Off.*) The hospital?
No thanks.

JUDE That's still a thing?

KYLE (*Off.*) Glad you're comfy going in a public toilet.
My train is not stopping at that station.

JUDE Thought you'd have gotten over that by now.

He opens the fridge.

Urgh, you stink.

KYLE (*Off.*) Excuse me?

JUDE Talking to the fridge.

KYLE (*Off.*) Thought you'd have gotten over that by now.

JUDE *flips his 'fuck you' finger towards the bathroom.*

(*Off.*) Heard that.

JUDE *takes pancetta, eggs, parmesan out the fridge.*

He closes the fridge door. Catches himself in the reflection.

A moment.

He gently touches his stitches.

JUDE Said it's quite common.

KYLE (*Off.*) Who did?

JUDE In the leaflet as well.
Spontaneous fainting.
Inadequate blood flow to the brain or something.

He flicks the kettle on.

KYLE (*Off.*) Need to look at your flush.

JUDE Kettle's on.

KYLE*'s back.*

KYLE Can look at it for you if you like?

JUDE It's working

KYLE Tried twice.

JUDE It's not working?

KYLE Just, wasn't, just pushed it down

JUDE Kyle, it's new it's –
pushed it down?

KYLE Twice.
Yes, I pushed it down.

JUDE You don't push it down
You lift it up.
Lift.
You don't *push.*
If you push, you'll

KYLE Lift, no, sure, yes

JUDE You said push.

KYLE No don't think so.
Lift.

Yes.
Lift.

,

I think.

JUDE Kyle.

KYLE I am so sorry.

JUDE Do you know how expensive?

KYLE Obviously I'll pay, going to pay.

JUDE Go on, guess, go on.

KYLE I don't know
Maybe…

JUDE It's a penthouse.

KYLE More expensive?

JUDE More floors, more piping, more –

KYLE Wasn't my fault.

JUDE Haven't seen you in… what? Eight? / Nine years?

KYLE Feel awful /

JUDE Almost a decade, and you've already broken –

KYLE Look, I'll try it again

JUDE Don't touch it.

KYLE Sorry.

,

Are you sure it's lift?

JUDE ,

Look at you.

JUDE *laughs*.

KYLE What?

JUDE You're so cute.

KYLE ?

JUDE ,

KYLE Fuck you.

JUDE Sorry I couldn't help myself.
Your face.
Priceless.

KYLE So it's not…

JUDE Not installed yet, no.

KYLE You're a penis.

JUDE The guy's sorting it Monday.

KYLE You knew, you knew I'd feel awful

JUDE You're adorable when you're scared.
You'd have licked the seat clean if I'd asked.
Lick, lick, lick.

KYLE Fuck you.

JUDE You're the first guest.

KYLE Want me to fill out a survey?

JUDE Stop being a cunt and compliment my bathroom.

KYLE Four.

JUDE Out of ten? You're going to shit on my face and give me a four out of ten?

KYLE There's no flush.

JUDE It's new.
It's a work-in-progress.

KYLE 'New Bog'
'Flushes Sold Separately'

JUDE Should've seen it before.

KYLE Bad?

JUDE	Terracotta.
KYLE	The bog?
JUDE	Doing this room next.
KYLE	Renovating?
JUDE	That's the rules. First you cry for six weeks Then you move into a really fucking expensive flat in Canary Wharf And then Because that won't quite fill the void You gut the place and start over.
KYLE	Think it's nice. Posh as fuck.
JUDE	Not that posh.
KYLE	If I clap twice, do the lights go out?
	He tries it.
JUDE	Yeah, not *that* posh.
	KYLE *looks at an ornament.*
KYLE	This is / posh.
JUDE	Please don't –
	KYLE *picks it up.*
	Okay, you're touching.
KYLE	Seems
JUDE	Expensive.
KYLE	Bold.
	,
	Looks a bit like a
JUDE	It's not.
KYLE	Like a [butt plug]

JUDE Not really.

KYLE Looks like it.

JUDE Oooh erm
Just

KYLE She's got heft.

JUDE Just
Be careful, yeah?

KYLE She's hefty.

JUDE It's porcelain.

KYLE Porcelain butt plug

JUDE Put it down.

KYLE Now that's fucking posh.

JUDE Come on, Kyle.

KYLE I'm not going to break it.

JUDE It's art.

KYLE Artwork. For your arse.

JUDE Careful.

KYLE Arsework.

JUDE Have you finished now?

KYLE Will you relax?
You're in knots.
So tight.
Need to loosen up.

He waves the ornament at JUDE. *Laughs.*

JUDE *shoots him a look.*

KYLE *puts it down.*

No, okay.
Sure.
It's art. I'm invested.

Who's the artist?

Barbara Hepworth?
Henry Moore?

,

Victoria Secret?

He laughs.

JUDE ,

It's Sam's.

Silence.

KYLE I'm so… [sorry]

JUDE No no it's… [fine]

KYLE Didn't realise

JUDE Not like he's going to mind, is he?

He laughs. It's nervous laughter.

Silence.

,

Sam's *sculpture.*
Not his butt plug.
It's not his butt plug.

KYLE No
No, of course.
I didn't think [it was] –

JUDE No.
Okay.

Silence.

Bought it at this charity thing.
Some young artist he probably fancied.

Silence.

Does look a bit butt-pluggy, doesn't it?

JUDE *goes into the kitchen, takes out some onions, starts to chop them.* KYLE *stays fixed on the ornament.*

Weird, you know.
Seeing you in my living room.

KYLE Is it?

JUDE (*Chopping.*) They've got an association
Do you know that?

,

National Onions Association.

,

I googled it.
Even got an acronym
'NOA'

'NOA.' Ha.

Now *that's* posh.

He laughs.

They've got some decent recipes on there.

Once you get past all that
All the fucking
batshit pseudo-science fucking
Onion mythology.
The healing powers of the onion et cetera.

,

It's funny. All the the… phytochemicals
The shit that makes you cry
Turns out that's the good stuff.
The healthy chemicals, the stuff that helps you fight diseases.
What Doesn't Kill You, you know.

Thought that was quite funny.

(*Not looking up.*) Don't you think that's funny?

KYLE (*Not really listening.*) Yeah.

,

Huh?

JUDE Read that on NOA.

KYLE What's that?

JUDE Got this whole section on how *not* to cry
How to 'cut the onion properly'
How to put in the freezer for half an hour before
Like a ritual
Preparing some religious fucking sacrifice.

Easier to just cry it out, I think.

KYLE I was going to send a message.

Silence.

When it happened.

People were leaving stuff on your Facebook wall.

I typed something out actually.
Deleted it before I sent.
Seemed a bit tacky.

JUDE Some people just don't know how to react.
It's safe.
You know what they say

KYLE What's that?

JUDE If you don't know how to speak to someone, post it on Facebook.

Can't break up with someone? Facebook.
Can't come out to your dad? Facebook.

KYLE Can't tell your landlord you stained the carpet.

JUDE Engaged?

KYLE Facebook.

JUDE Pregnant?

KYLE Facebook.

JUDE Circumcised?

KYLE Instagram.

They laugh.

Silence.

KYLE I am really / [sorry] –

JUDE Don't.

If I had a pound every time someone said the word 'condolences'…

,

You know when you say a word too many times it just loses all its meaning?

Your ears just disassociate?

JUDE *clears his throat.*

Condolences, condolences, condolences, condolences, condolences, condolences, condolences…

KYLE *catches on after a while, joins in.*

KYLE Condolences, / condolences, condolences, condolences, condolences, condolences, condolences…

JUDE Condolences, / condolences, condolences, condolences, condolences, condolences…

They keep going. It starts to become messy. They aren't making any sense. They can't help but laugh.

JUDE *laughs, until he doesn't.*

He's fighting back tears.

(*Sniffling.*) Fucking hate onions.

He buries himself in a cupboard.

(*Rummaging.*) What do you fancy?
There's some in here somewhere.

He pulls out a bottle of Merlot.

Here it is.

KYLE Oh.
Erm
I'm not –
I don't really drink any more.

JUDE Oh.

,

Sure.

KYLE You can have one if you want.

JUDE I don't really either.

KYLE I'm not judging.

JUDE Just keep a bottle for when people come over.
Thought you might…

KYLE Right.

JUDE But you don't.

KYLE I haven't touched anything.

JUDE No.

KYLE Just think
Best to be all in or all out, you know.
Especially how we were.

JUDE Me too.

KYLE So I haven't.
Not even alcohol.

JUDE Me neither.

KYLE Right.

,

You haven’t taken anything since?

JUDE Is that surprising?

KYLE Didn’t know that you’d
Given it all up.
Thought you’d still be in the scene.

JUDE I was.
For a bit.
Things change.

KYLE Yeah.

JUDE Things changed with Sam.
Realised it didn’t have to be like that.
I used to think that was life. That was what Queer Culture was. Drugs and alcohol and parties. Thought it was just what you did, how you socialised, how you had sex. That was how you were meant to feel all the time.

Silence.

KYLE Do you miss it?

JUDE I’m a different person now.

KYLE I know I shouldn’t say this
But we were hot.

I look back
And think, wow.
We looked fucking hot.
My body.

JUDE Probably because we hadn’t eaten for five days.

KYLE Everyone loved us.
It was good.
Sometimes.

JUDE *resumes chopping.*

,

I heard about an incident.

A moment.

JUDE Incident?

KYLE A few months after we broke up.

JUDE From who?

KYLE That you'd…

JUDE Was it Harry?

KYLE No.

JUDE You still speak to that lot?

KYLE I told you, it wasn't –

JUDE I'm not ashamed.

Silence.

KYLE Well, you look really well now. And you've got this great place so.
Whatever you did, it obviously worked.

JUDE Is that a joke?

KYLE Not really, / no.

JUDE It's a bit of a shitty Joke, Kyle.

KYLE I meant it genuinely
I mean…
What I meant was…

Sorry.

JUDE Okay.

,

Well,

,

I haven't since, so…

JUDE *starts dabbing the stitches on his forehead.*

KYLE Don't, don't /

JUDE No, I know.

KYLE Touching it, shouldn't keep

JUDE Scratchy
Is that, is it normal, it's / scratchy?

KYLE Don't scratch it, don't

JUDE Wasn't
Just saying it *is* stratchy.
Doesn't mean I *was scratching.*

KYLE You were.

JUDE I'm not.
I've stopped.
I wasn't.

Silence.

JUDE *begins making a carbonara. Caramelising onions, frying bacon, cracking and whisking eggs, all the good stuff. He's half in the conversation and half in the carbonara.*

KYLE*'s phone buzzes.*

KYLE Should probably flush the –

JUDE I'll sort it later.

KYLE It's a number two.

Don't want it to… fester.

His phone buzzes again.

JUDE Mr Popular tonight, aren't you.

KYLE Huh?

And again.

JUDE Said you must be popular.

KYLE Like a big bucket
You know?

Like a mop bucket
Or like a big pan, big saucepan

JUDE I'll get it

KYLE It's my number two.
I'll do it.

JUDE I'm happy. I'm happy to do it.

KYLE He's happy to do it.

JUDE …

KYLE He is.

JUDE Ooh Imma Stab.

KYLE He's happy to do it.

JUDE Imma stab stab stab you.

KYLE Thought he was happy?

JUDE Okay stop.
Just
Stop. Okay?

KYLE He won't let anyone help him.
He's too stubborn.

JUDE You make me sound like a crusty old queen.

KYLE He's angry.

JUDE I've never found that funny, you know.

You'd do it to each other, your wanky art friends would lap it up. You thought you were so fucking funny –

KYLE It was funny –

JUDE You looked like a twat.

KYLE I've changed.

JUDE Now you're a twat with a moustache.

KYLE You barely even recognised me when I turned up.

JUDE I didn't know you were coming.
Thought I'd passed out again. Like I was dreaming or in the afterlife or something.

KYLE I did tell them
On the phone
I said
Are you sure I'm still the emergency contact?

JUDE Would've been Sam.
Don't think I've updated it.

KYLE I assumed.

JUDE Probably still on the system
Previous emergency contact.
It was you when I joined.

KYLE On the phone they said
Jude's in A&E
Can you go and pick him up.

Was driving when they said that.
Almost hit a fox.

Silence.

JUDE Still got that god-awful leopard-print suitcase.
That hasn't changed, has it?

KYLE What?

JUDE In the back of your car.
I could see it poking out the back.

KYLE It's nice
It's a nice size.

JUDE Thought
Fuck me, he's still lugging that old girl around.

KYLE Leopard print is a neutral.

JUDE Okay then.

KYLE It is!

They laugh.

Silence.

JUDE I never knew you could grow a…

Gestures.

[moustache.]

KYLE Yeah. Me neither
But

Ta-dah!

JUDE I always said you'd suit some hair.
Makes you look quite different.
Older.

KYLE More mature, I think.

JUDE No. Older.

KYLE You didn't recognise me.

JUDE Haven't seen you since you 'disappeared'.

KYLE Disappeared?

JUDE Turned around and
Poof!
Gone.
Cinderella has vanished from the ball.

KYLE Here we go.

JUDE What?

KYLE Nothing.

JUDE Go on.

KYLE It was almost a decade ago.

JUDE You abandoned me.

KYLE Didn't 'abandon' you, that's
Okay, that's going / a bit far.

JUDE That's how I felt.

KYLE That's not an 'I' statement.
'You abandoned me'
An accusation, not a feeling.

JUDE Okay.
I felt abandoned, by you.

KYLE 'Abandoned.' Right.

JUDE Back then, yes.
That's how I felt.

KYLE I guess I don't remember it like that.

JUDE Don't do that.
Don't gaslight me like that.

KYLE We broke up and I didn't come back.
That's not 'disappearing'.
That's not 'abandoning' you.

JUDE Stop it.

KYLE What?

JUDE Picking out the words I've said
Stretching them out
Like you're mocking me.

KYLE That's not my intention.

JUDE The way you're saying 'abandoned'
Like I'm a four-year-old.

KYLE If that's how you're interpreting what I'm / saying…

JUDE How I'm *interpreting*?
Not what you're saying. God fucking forbid it's what you're saying.
No, no.
It's *me*.

KYLE That's not fair.

JUDE (*Cont.*) Misinterpreting you.

KYLE I don't think it's fair, actually, that I've sort of come here trying to help you, trying to be helpful, and now I'm being accused / of

JUDE Not accusing / –

KYLE Making you feel this way, making you feel… which is actually quite horrible, actually, and I'm supposed to sit here and agree with that? Well, I'm sorry, but I don't.

Silence.

JUDE You could have responded to my texts.
You could've said something.

Together for nearly two years.
We have one argument, and you're gone.
Off the grid.

I had to call your mum.

I didn't know if you were dead.

Silence.

KYLE I didn't want to go back to that.
Put myself in that position.

JUDE What position?

KYLE I was doing well. Fine. Was doing fine.

JUDE You weren't there.

KYLE I'm very sorry about that, all that
But I'm not responsible
For your recovery.

JUDE I needed you.

KYLE I was going through my own process.
Recovering. Healing. Avoiding things that
I would have found triggering.

JUDE Triggering?

KYLE Keep putting myself in those situations, hanging around people who were using.
All your friends.

JUDE *Our* friends.

KYLE They were always really *your* friends.

JUDE You didn't like our friends?

KYLE Just
Needed new air.

JUDE *starts to undress himself.*

JUDE Was I a trigger?

,

Kyle?

He moves sharply.

Ah ah ah

He holds his wrist.

KYLE What's happened, what's –

JUDE Ouch –

KYLE What is it?
what's painful?

JUDE My arm it's
Ah ah.

KYLE Stay still.
Just be still for a second.

JUDE It's the shirt it's –

KYLE Okay –

JUDE It's all –

KYLE Take it off.

JUDE I'm fine.

KYLE Do you want me to?

JUDE I can do it.

Goes to take his left arm out its sleeve.

He can't do it.

KYLE You're going too fast.

Hey.

Be careful.
The doctor said be careful.

Okay, Stop.
You'll hurt yourself more.

KYLE *takes over. He helps* JUDE *out the sleeve.*

Then out his shirt.

Then out his trousers.

He knows his way around JUDE*'s body. He's been here before.*

A moment.

They look at each other close enough to kiss.
They don't, but they both know they could.

Should really think about…

JUDE Oh.

KYLE Making a move.

JUDE Right. No.
Of course.

,

There's pasta if you…

He fills a pan with water from the kettle.

KYLE Gotta drive back.

JUDE Okay.

KYLE Only came up to make sure you were okay.
Didn't want you collapsing in the lift.

JUDE Right.

Well
I'm okay, so.

KYLE Painkillers are on the counter. I've put them on the [counter]
The ones they gave you.

JUDE Yes.

KYLE Don't take these one on an empty stomach
But these ones, you can take whenever
If you feel bad / in the night.

JUDE Yes, yes
I know.
I got the full TED Talk too.

KYLE Right, well.
Right.
I'll get my coat.

JUDE Back of the door.

KYLE Okay.

JUDE Thank you for driving. Helping me up here.

KYLE No no it's
Honestly. It's been… to see you.

JUDE Took ten years and accident and emergency to finally get you here, but

Thanks.

,

I didn't really have anyone else, so

A moment.

Are you sure you don't want any food?

KYLE I didn't bring a coat.

JUDE Sorry?

KYLE No, didn't bring one.

JUDE Why didn't you bring one?

KYLE I'll be fine once I'm in the car.

JUDE Wait here.

He disappears into the bedroom.

KYLE I'm fine
Don't worry about –
Jude.

JUDE (*Off.*) It's freezing outside.

KYLE I thought you were meant to be the fun one.

He's back, holding a jacket.

JUDE I'll find a scarf as well.
Hang on.

KYLE (*Re: jacket.*) There's one in the car.

JUDE Don't be stupid, Kyle.
Just… put it on, come on.

KYLE I'm not cold.

JUDE You can keep it.
Don't have to worry about, you know…
returning it.

KYLE I can't wear this.
It won't fit me.

JUDE ,

Because it's…?

KYLE Because it's…
No.
Because –

JUDE — You'll strut a leopard-print suitcase through Heathrow Terminal Two but you won't wear my jacket to the car?

KYLE — This is ridiculous.
I didn't park in the Antarctic.
I'm across the road.

They look at each other.

A moment.

JUDE*'s suddenly aware he's only in his socks, vest and underpants.*

What?

JUDE — Oi.

KYLE — What?

JUDE — Don't look at me like that.

KYLE — Not looking at you.

JUDE — I'm naked.

KYLE — You're not *naked.*

JUDE — My titties are out.
You can see through [the vest].

KYLE — No you can't.

JUDE — You're looking.

KYLE — I'm not.

JUDE — There.
Right then. You just did.
You're looking at my tit.

KYLE — What?

JUDE — Just glanced down. Right now.
I saw you.

KYLE — Stop being a slut and put some clothes on.

JUDE Help me.
I mean.
Before you go.

KYLE Getting dressed?

JUDE I can't really.
With my arm, I'll get knotty.

KYLE Some joggers or something?

JUDE In the bedroom.

He goes off to the bedroom.

KYLE (*Off.*) What top?

JUDE Something loose.

KYLE (*Off.*) Hoodie?

JUDE On the radiator

KYLE (*Off.*) I see it.

Beat.

JUDE You keeping him then?

KYLE*'s back.*

KYLE What's that?

JUDE Freddie Mercury.

KYLE (*Touching his moustache.*) You like it?

KYLE*'s phone buzzes. Another message.*

JUDE Give me my clothes, Kyle.

He does.

KYLE (*Re: moustache.*) Might trim him back at bit.

His phone buzzes again. And again.

JUDE You sure you don't want to answer that?

KYLE What?

JUDE Your phone. It keeps –

And again.

KYLE Oh, no. It's not, it's
Work WhatsApp.

JUDE ,

At three a.m.?

KYLE The freelance dream.

JUDE *tries to put the hoodie on. Struggles.*

Boss keeps me on a short leash and a tight deadline.

JUDE (*Re: hoodie.*) Kyle?

KYLE *weaves the hoodie over* JUDE*'s head, guides his arm through.*

KYLE *picks up the bloody shirt.*

KYLE I'll pop this in the bin.

JUDE I'll throw it in the washing machine.
It's just a bit of blood.

KYLE It won't come out.

JUDE *drops the spaghetti into the pan of water.*

JUDE It's expensive.
It's a nice shirt.

KYLE You own more than one shirt, Jude.

JUDE It's T.M.Lewin.
I'll put it in the wash, it'll come right out. Will be good as new tomorrow.

KYLE Not tomorrow, no.
Probably best not tomorrow.

JUDE Sorry?

KYLE Don't want to overdo it.

JUDE Just taken two weeks' bereavement.
They need me in.

KYLE Take a few days off.
That's what the doctor said.
Just until / – [you're better]

JUDE I have clients.

KYLE Sure they'll understand.

JUDE I'm in international shipping law.
My 'clients' are countries.

KYLE We talked about it and said she'll sort all that.

JUDE Who?

KYLE Jenny… I think?

JUDE You called my boss?

KYLE The paramedic said you should take / some time off.

JUDE You can't do that.
You can't call my boss.
You called my boss?

KYLE She called me, actually.

JUDE Jesus Christ.

KYLE Checking in, how you were.
This woman called Jenny.

JUDE I know who Jenny is, Kyle.

KYLE She suggested /

JUDE Did she? /

KYLE I told her what they said
What the hospital recommended
And Jenny suggested –
Jenny suggested and I agreed
That it would be good for you to take some space.

JUDE That's good.
That's nice you've got a little…

Gestures.

	…You know A little…
	Thing
	Going on. You and Jenny.
KYLE	Once you feel better / you can –
JUDE	I'm fine. Feeling much better.
KYLE	Once you're properly better.
JUDE	Look. Woohoo. I'm great. I'm amazing. I'm walking on sunshine.
KYLE	She was going to contact the… Is it the board, or something? I want to say the board
JUDE	I should call. I'll call back.
KYLE	To explain what's happened.
JUDE	Call and check in with Jen.
KYLE	It's half three in the morning.
JUDE	Text her, then. Tell her I'll see her tomorrow.
KYLE	She's already sorted it.
JUDE	Where's my phone?
KYLE	Maybe wait out the day tomorrow. Reassess.
JUDE	Is it in my trouser pocket? I think it's in the pocket.
KYLE	Have a pyjama day. Do a puzzle

JUDE Can you look?

KYLE Remember that puzzle of like
The gay penguin jigsaw
Your grandad bought it for us.
Never bloody finished it.

JUDE Pass my phone, Kyle.

KYLE Months later
We found that whole bag
A whole fucking bag of pieces
Just left in the box –

JUDE I can't do that
I can't, I can't, can't do that
Can't stay here
The loneliest fucking loneliest place
Please
Fucking
Please let me go to work.

KYLE Alright, okay okay. Hey.

Hey hey, come here.

Sh sh sh.
Okay. You're okay.

He moves over to JUDE, *holds him.*

Silence.

After a moment, JUDE *goes back to the carbonara.*

KYLE *goes over to the bin. It's a flush rectangular stainless-steel one with a fancy foot pedal.*

Goes to drop the shirt in. Stops.

He reaches into the bin and pulls out a cashmere suit jacket. Then another white shirt.

Throughout the next, KYLE *continues to pull out various suit-wear. Blazers, ties, trousers, shirts.*

Maybe even shoes. As much as could fit in a bin. Apart from creasing, they're all in immaculate condition.

JUDE (*Cooking.*) It was his favourite, you know.
Sam would take his clients to these dinners, these fancy fuck-off restaurants in The City

Then he'd come home and make himself a dirty bowl of spaghetti carbonara. With onions.

Fucking psychopath.

KYLE I think T.M.Lewin vomited in your bin.

JUDE *looks round.*

JUDE Hello, Mister Fox.
You know that's considered rude in some places?
Scavenging through someone's bin.

KYLE Are you throwing these away?

JUDE Washing machine's broken.

KYLE Jesus
You're just
Throwing your clothes away?

JUDE The guy's sorting it.
Coming next week.

KYLE Yeah?
How many weeks you been saying that?

,

This is expensive shit, Jude.

,

Jude?

He looks at JUDE.

Stop
You're still doing it.

JUDE Doing what?

KYLE Stop touching.

JUDE I'm not. I'm just –

KYLE Knew someone who ended up pulling them out.
His stitches.

JUDE Not going to pull them out.

KYLE Kept scratching and then eventually
Just unravelled, like shoelaces, dangling.

JUDE *stirs the spaghetti. Maybe tries a bit. It's not al dente yet.*

JUDE There's three minutes on that
Three minutes max.

KYLE He's got permanent scarring now.
Can still see it, just here, on his forehead.

JUDE (*Holding his tummy.*) Did you hear that?

KYLE It was a bad fall.
They said it was a pretty bad.

JUDE My belly. Did you just hear that?
I'm fucking rumbling.

KYLE Where's the leaflet?

JUDE (*Cont.*) Three Billy Goats Gruff over here.

KYLE I just need to find the
Where is it?
Where the hell is –
It's here!
Got it.
It was in my *back* pocket.

JUDE Hank Marvin.

KYLE (*Reading.*) 'Fainting often results when blood flow to the brain…'
Yadda yadda yadda…

'…as a result of stress, grief, overheating… fainting may also occur after taking certain medications' –

Where is it? Where's the –

(*Reading.*) 'Patient is to avoid any unnecessary physical endeavour, unnecessary, erm, unnecessary'…

JUDE I'm making a carbonara, Kyle.
I'm not touching the fucking void.

KYLE 'Unnecessary… INCLUDING'
Right, here we go
'Including standardised household chores and activities.'
So
Pass it over.

JUDE What?

KYLE I'll finish it.

JUDE Thought you were leaving.

KYLE*'s phone buzzes. Another message.*

He pulls it out, glances at it, then puts it away.

Everything okay?

KYLE It's half three in the morning. I'll survive three more minutes.

JUDE No, honestly, go. I'm fine on my own.
Not even using my left arm.
Look.
Look at me.
Go.

KYLE He can't do it

JUDE Can't do what?

KYLE He can't let go.

JUDE Don't.

KYLE (*Laughing.*) Sorry.

He stops laughing.

Sorry.

,

Just wanna help.

JUDE I know.

Maybe try
Hmm
Be a little forceful

KYLE Forceful?

JUDE No, not forceful.
Not force
But
Just be assertive

KYLE Right

JUDE Just demand that you are taking over.
Don't offer.
Just do it.

KYLE I can do assertive.

JUDE Go on.

KYLE Ready?

JUDE I'm ready.

KYLE *clears his throat.*

KYLE Jude.

JUDE Yes?

KYLE Jude.

JUDE Yes, Kyle?

KYLE I need you to stop cooking now.

JUDE And why's that?

KYLE Because I'm taking over.
I'm
I'm going to take over now.
So you need to step away.

A moment.

JUDE *starts laughing.*

It's not funny.

JUDE No no it's not.
I'm not.

KYLE Don't laugh.

JUDE You're not defusing a bomb.

KYLE That wasn't what I was going for.

JUDE No, course.

KYLE Thought I did quite well.

JUDE No no you did, baby.
You did well.

He hands over the kitchen tongs.

KYLE Wow.
Is this really happening?

JUDE Don't piss on it.
Don't piss the moment.

KYLE *holds them like he's holding an award.*

KYLE Wow this is really
Gosh. Erm –

JUDE Okay cool you're pissing on the moment.

KYLE Thank you so much, wow.
Firstly, I'd like to thank the academy
And my agent, of course.
Like to thank my mum
If you're / watching at home.

JUDE Right up the wall
Covering it / in piss

KYLE Most of all
Shush.
Most of all
I'd like to thank this man right here
For giving me the opportunity

JUDE It's overcooking

KYLE Don't do that.

JUDE Stop it boiling

KYLE You can't interrupt a man during his acceptance speech.

JUDE Because the way you do it
Look.
You need to drop the pasta into that pan
Yep
With the bacon
Water
Add some water
Uh-huh.

KYLE *does.*

Yeah
Now mix it. Toss.
Gently.

KYLE *does.*

That's it.
That's better

JUDE *picks up the whisked eggs.*

KYLE Hey –

JUDE I'm not doing anything.
Don't look at me. I'm invisible.

KYLE Sit down.

JUDE Now it's ready just /
Pour this into –

KYLE I know that, I'm –
I know what / to do.

JUDE Delicately.
I don't want egg-fried noodles

KYLE Go.
GO.

JUDE I'm sitting, I'm sitting.
Look.

A moment.

KYLE *adds the eggs. Stirs. Tosses.*

JUDE *watches.*

KYLE Stop it.

JUDE What?

KYLE Stop.

JUDE I haven't –
What? What have I done?
Am I *sitting* wrong?
Oh, sorry, Caravaggio
I didn't realise you wanted my side profile!
Gosh, you shoulda just said.

KYLE Like you're back-seat driving, like you're

JUDE Not doing anything

KYLE Can feel your eyes
Watching.
Watching, watching.

JUDE I'm just sitting.

KYLE I can do this, you know.
I can make pasta.

JUDE I'm not even –
Not saying anything.

Silence.

KYLE We should do that thing where you eat in the dark.
You know those restaurants where you eat in the dark?
We should do that.

Claps twice, as if to turn the lights out.

Laughs.

Can't see what you're eating.
Might make you chill the fuck out.

,

Where do you keep your plates?

JUDE Haven't even tasted it.

KYLE I just know.
Sixth sense.

JUDE Use some salt.

KYLE Give me a chance.

KYLE *walks a fork-full of pasta over to* JUDE.

Sits beside him.

Blows on the pasta to cool it down.

KYLE *feeds* JUDE.

JUDE *chews. Swallows.*

A moment.

JUDE *kisses* KYLE.

KYLE *goes with it initially, then pulls away.*

A moment.

It needs more salt.

JUDE Come here.

KYLE No
I can't
I can't

JUDE Did I do something so –

KYLE No

JUDE Okay, I

KYLE Should
You know
Stir.
Not burn.

JUDE Kyle?

KYLE I'm sorry, I

JUDE I want this.

KYLE Do you have any salt?

JUDE If you think you're taking advantage
You're not.

KYLE (*Searching.*) Salt, salt, salt, salt…

JUDE I want you to.

KYLE Don't do that.
Don't put me in that position.

JUDE You don't want to?

KYLE …

JUDE Right.

Fuck.

Wow, did I just misread this whole…
Because I might have really misread this. Really got it wrong.

I thought you were…
Thought you wanted to.

KYLE Don't think you're in the best place
Best frame of mind

To make sensible choices
Right now.

JUDE — Well.
Wow.
I mean
This is a bit embarrassing, isn't it.

KYLE — We can just pretend that that…
That we didn't –

JUDE — Am I not attractive any more?

KYLE — What?

JUDE — Is that it?

KYLE — You're out of parmesan.

JUDE — Because I'm older?

KYLE — You weren't concentrating
Accidentally grated the whole block.

JUDE — Not even a pity fuck?
Not even a sympathy shag?
God. You can't even bring yourself to that.

KYLE — Sorry, I just, I really can't see the salt.
Is it this cupboard did you say?

JUDE — Maybe it's the grief
Making me unfuckable.

KYLE — Where's the salt?
Josh –
Jude?
Where have you / put it?

JUDE — Josh?

KYLE — Ah-ha.
Here it is.

JUDE — Who's Josh?

KYLE — Found it.

JUDE You just called me Josh.

KYLE Did I?

JUDE Josh.

KYLE No.

JUDE No?

KYLE No one.
I don't know, no I don't…

JUDE Right.

KYLE No, I do know, yes.

JUDE You do?

KYLE Yes

JUDE Who?

KYLE Josh.

JUDE Yeah?

KYLE This guy I've been…
We've been – we're sort of…

JUDE Oh.

KYLE Together.

JUDE ,

Oohh.

Beat.

KYLE Was going to say something.

JUDE You didn't have to.

KYLE I was going to.

JUDE Nothing to do with me.

KYLE No, but

JUDE You and Josh.

KYLE Yeah.

Ooh.

JUDE What?

KYLE No, nothing.

JUDE What?

KYLE Just a bit weird

JUDE What is?

KYLE You saying his name.
Quite weird, actually. Sounds quite weird.

JUDE Does it?

KYLE No.

But,
Yes.

JUDE Right.

KYLE Just does.

JUDE Okay

KYLE Don't know why.

JUDE Sorry.

KYLE Didn't expect it to.

Silence.

KYLE Do you want to eat?

JUDE Another 'J'

KYLE It's ready, it's

JUDE Kyle and Jude…
Kyle and Josh…

KYLE Oo, there you go again, saying his name

JUDE Whose name?

KYLE You don't know him.

JUDE Is that your ‘type’?

KYLE What?

JUDE Names that begin with J.

KYLE Don’t think that’s a ‘type’.

JUDE Would Josh think it’s a type?

KYLE Don’t do that.
Don’t say his name like you know him.

JUDE What are the chances?
We’re a dime a dozen, us Js.

KYLE Right.

JUDE Do you reckon he’d like me?

KYLE Erm

JUDE Would we get along?

KYLE You’re very different people.

JUDE Why not?

KYLE He’s Josh, and you’re…

JUDE Josh wouldn’t like me?

KYLE Different.

JUDE Josh.

KYLE Okay.

JUDE And Jude.

KYLE Huh?

JUDE Sounds like a TV show.
‘*Josh and Jude*’

KYLE Not really.

JUDE Netflix Original.

KYLE Don’t think so.

JUDE Someone’s getting jumpy.

KYLE I'm not.

JUDE Oo, there you go.
Jumpy, jumpy.

KYLE I'm not rising to it.

JUDE Maybe that's the name of your next boyfriend

Jude.
Josh.
Jumpy.

KYLE Watch me not rise.

JUDE Does Josh know you're here?

KYLE Stop saying his name.

JUDE And you're having some pasta
And it's all very platonic

KYLE Yes.

JUDE And he'll be happy to believe that?

KYLE Yes

JUDE Great.

,

That's good.

Silence.

He sounds nice.

KYLE He is.

Silence.

JUDE Was it on Grindr?

KYLE No.

JUDE Josh wasn't on Grindr?

KYLE No.
I don't know.
I don't think so.

JUDE That's how people meet, isn't it?

KYLE Do you really want to talk about this?
I mean
I don't want to talk about this.
I know we're not together any more
But it just feels

JUDE No, okay.

KYLE Doesn't it?

JUDE Sure.

Silence.

Was it the lido?

KYLE That's how *we* met.

JUDE Did we?

KYLE You know we did.

JUDE You didn't meet Josh at the lido?

KYLE Why would we have met at the lido?

JUDE You've got a track record of meeting guys at the lido
So, you know
Statistically it's possible, in fact highly probable that you would have met him at the lido

KYLE He's my publisher.

JUDE Oh.

,

Right.

,

(*Re: phone.*) Short leash tight deadline, huh.

,

Didn't know you'd been… [published]

KYLE Publishing assistant, he's –

JUDE I keep a look-out in Foyles.

KYLE I'm doing children's literature at the moment.

JUDE Oh.

KYLE The money's good.

JUDE What about fantasy?

KYLE Yeah, still do.
Sometimes.

JUDE But there's no money in that or?

KYLE There is, yes, of course
There's money in it.
But fantasy, you know, there's
It's more competitive.
It's a lot of talented people.

JUDE You are talented.

KYLE I don't mind children's literature.

JUDE What's that then?
Farm animals?

KYLE What's wrong with farm animals?

JUDE You're a fantasy-fiction illustrator.

KYLE I'm an illustrator.
I do lots of things.
I'm versatile.

JUDE Farm animals.

KYLE All types of animals.

JUDE That's versatile.

KYLE It's well-respected.
You're on the front.
'Illustrations by Kyle Bannerman'
You don't always get that on other stuff.

JUDE And that makes it worthwhile?

KYLE We don't all need the penthouse version of everything.

JUDE What's that supposed to mean?

KYLE I like what I'm doing.

JUDE Okay.

KYLE I do.

JUDE I believe you.

Silence.

KYLE I do.

Silence.

JUDE And he publishes them, your farm animals?

KYLE Publishing assistant.
Yeah.
He's…
Yeah.

,

Not for much longer.
He's got a new job now.

Big international publishing house.
Dream job for him.

JUDE Wow.
Well done Josh.

KYLE Yeah.

It's great.

,

It's in Singapore.

JUDE Fuck.

KYLE Yeah.

JUDE So you're both… [going]?

KYLE Yeah.

JUDE Wow.

,

Congratulations.

KYLE Thanks.

JUDE When do you… / [go]?

KYLE Tomorrow.
Well today now, I suppose.

Silence.

JUDE You hate big cities.

You always talked about moving away after uni.

KYLE I don't think so.

JUDE What are you going to do?
Have you got a job.

KYLE I can draw anywhere.

JUDE So you're just going to go?
Just up and out.
Leave everything.

KYLE That's what you do.
When you love someone.

You give things up.

Silence.

JUDE Cute, that's

KYLE We don't have to –

JUDE Are your parents happy?

KYLE Let's not do this.

JUDE Your mum must be.

KYLE I don't want to have this conversation.

JUDE Bet she can't wait to visit.

KYLE Don't have to talk
About our… 'lives'

JUDE We talked about Sam.

KYLE That's different.

JUDE How?

KYLE Don't really want to talk about my…
Talk about…
You know…

,

And if you want to talk about your…
Your… 'love life'
You know
That's fine.
I'm happy to do that, but –

JUDE You're right.
No, you're right.

We don't have to
You know
Talk
Or whatever
We don't have to do that if you don't want.

It's not any of my
Not really
Not anything to do with me.

KYLE That's okay, that's

JUDE We'll just
Sit here.

And not talk about him. Your boyfriend.

Silence.

KYLE ,

Husband.

Silence.

JUDE Oh.

KYLE Yeah.

JUDE Right.

A long silence.

,

You're not wearing a ring.

,

Why aren't you wearing a ring?

KYLE What?

JUDE Where is it? The ring.

KYLE We don't really…
believe
in all that.

All that stuff around it, it's not really our thing.

JUDE It's a wedding ring.

Not your GCSE options, it's not multiple choice.

It's part of it, it's an an emblem of, not an emblem, but yes, a a a an emblem of love through time, a symbol of devotion, an agreement between two parties to love and cherish one another for the rest of their lives for the rest of their –

And that's just marriage on the tin. That's just your bog-standard ring. Anyone can wear that, any Adam and Eve.

Your ring, it's fucking…
It's colossal. Represents hundreds of people rioting, rallying, to be treated as human beings, their human rights
The right to *love someone else.*
It's that.
And it's death, it's

KYLE Death?

JUDE Fighting and losing and fighting again
And
Even more than that
Even more
It's love.

It's fucking love and it's equality. It's fairness and it's justice. It's fucking justice, that's what it is, Kyle. It's fairness and it's justice and it's love
And it's a pretty good fucking indicator of knowing who you should and shouldn't kiss.

Silence.

KYLE I'm –

JUDE But that's
You know
Fuck all that, right?
Why bother?
Fuck Stonewall and New Orleans and Orlando.
Fuck the entire homo-fucking-history of marriage equality
Because, you know
You
Don't Really Believe In All That.

Silence.

KYLE Should've said before.

JUDE Would've been good.

KYLE Yeah.

Silence.

JUDE *goes to the cupboard. Takes out a bottle of Merlot.*

He pours a glass.

I thought you weren't drinking

JUDE I thought you weren't married
But hey
Look at us.
Full of little mysteries.

JUDE *downs the whole glass, then pours another.*

He looks at KYLE.

What?

Is there something on my face?

He laughs. Touches his stitches.

Three fucking weeks. Jesus.

I think I need one of those collars. Those cones, Like a dog. You know those cones, those see-through cones for dogs?

He laughs. KYLE *doesn't.*

Hungry?

JUDE *goes into the kitchen and takes the pan of carbonara. He comes back and sits on the floor opposite* KYLE.

A moment.

He starts to eat with his hands. His speech is punctuated by gulps of red wine. His mouth always half-full.

Don't want any?

Silence.

Sure?

KYLE *doesn't respond. He's staring at* JUDE.

You know it's fucking weird when you do this.

Silence.

JUDE *stares back, trying to outstare him.*

,

Nope,
Not doing it.
Sorry this is too weird.

Silence.

You're being creepy, you know that?
It's scary.
You're scary.

Silence.

What's wrong?

Whose assassination are you planning?
Let me in.

Kyle?

Silence.

Okay.

If you don't have anything to say, best get going.
Don't want to miss your flight.

Leopard-print suitcase.
Singapore isn't ready for you, babe.

He laughs.

Silence.

Stop trying to look like you're looking through me
Like you're some fucking X-ray machine

What's inside, Kyle?
What can you see?

KYLE*'s phone starts ringing.*

A moment.

Ooooh.

(*To the phone.*) Hello.

,

You gonna get that?

KYLE *doesn't flinch.*

It rings.

And rings.

JUDE *finishes another glass.*

It stops ringing.

JUDE *pours some more.*

(*Re: phone.*) He gone now, so…

,

No, I understand.
Probably best.

,

Might sniff you out.

,

Smell it over the phone.

,

Don't want to upset little Joshy.

JUDE *laughs.* KYLE *doesn't.*

A joke.

No need to get all… cagey, all…

,

I've gotten into your head.
See.

,

We're celebrating.
Aren't we?
Bon Voyage et cetera.

He takes the bottle…

Pours KYLE *a glass.*

In case you change your mind.

JUDE *dims the lights.*

Shall we put some music on?

JUDE *crawls over to the speaker. He puts on some music.*

He starts twerking.

How's this for foxy?

JUDE *continues dancing on the floor.*

S'il vous plaît, Monsieur
Can I have this dance?

Oui?

Non?

JUDE *returns to the pan of pasta.*

He looks at KYLE.

Okay can you stop now.
I'm serious. Stop it.
It's scaring me.

Kyle.

Kyle.

He eats another fistful of spaghetti.

This is disgusting.

He laughs.

Try some.
It's fucking rank.
I burnt the onions.
Try it.

He takes a handful and extends his arm, offering it to KYLE.

A moment.

Nothing.

Silence.

JUDE *flings the handful of pasta at* KYLE.

KYLE What the fuck, Jude.

JUDE What do you think?

He takes another handful and lobs it at him.

KYLE What the fuck are you doing?

JUDE Can you taste it?

KYLE Look at my top.
Jesus Christ
Look what you've done to my top.

JUDE *throws another fistful.*

KYLE Fucking stop.

JUDE *laughs.*

JUDE Fuck, that tastes bad.

KYLE *walks over and turns off the music.*

KYLE I'm not doing this.

JUDE Rwarrr
Look who's getting foxy / now.

KYLE Enough.
No games.
Just for one fucking minute.

He snaps the lights back up. The temperature changes.

KYLE How did you fall?

JUDE Like a sack of potatoes.

KYLE I need a moment of real.
Right now.
Okay?

JUDE That's what they said.
The fifth-floor guys.

KYLE Jude.

JUDE They said I was just standing there
On the fifth floor
Waiting for the printer to print
And slipped.
Nicked my head on the corner of the printer on my way down.
Landed on my arm.

KYLE *grabs the vase off the shelf.*

Don't touch that.
Kyle.

KYLE What's in the vase?

JUDE We've already had this.
Don't touch my shit

KYLE Shall we / find out?

JUDE Put it / down now.

KYLE Let's fucking / find out.

JUDE Kyle –

KYLE *goes to smash the vase.*

JUDE *grabs it from him before he does.*

Is this your attempt at an intervention?

KYLE ‘Fainting may also occur after taking certain medications.’
That’s what it says.
That’s what the leaflet says.

JUDE OH.
‘Medications’
Oh fuck.
Oh right.
Of course.
Well done you, Inspector Clouseau!

KYLE I’m not judging you.

JUDE I suppose you didn’t weigh it?

KYLE If you think I’m judging you, if that’s how you’re interpreting / this –

JUDE Because if you’d have weighed it…
If you were really
Going full-out with the whole
Detective thing
You would’ve weighed it.

One gram. Methamphetamine.

All there.

Not been touched, so.

,

Do you have one of those
You know
One of those magnifying…

He mimes looking through a magnifying glass.

A pocket one, maybe?
Maybe if we look in your pockets?

That’s a shame.
Would’ve really made the whole…

Aesthetic. Wouldn’t it.

Silence.

JUDE *takes the baggie from* KYLE.

I asked around.
No I didn't
I asked Antony
And if anyone was going to judge me, it would probably be Antony
But Antony's in IT.
So fuck what he thinks.

And he said there's this guy and he hosts sometimes.
He's quite expensive. Sixty.

The stuff's good
And this hybrid phase of mixing and diluting is getting more and more popular so, you know, you've got to be careful
He doesn't do that, he's all the pure stuff.
So I go down one night
He's throwing a party
It's been going a day or so by the time I get there
And it's heaving.
There's about six guys in the first room and they're all fucking each other.
Naked. Except they've all kept their socks on.
And I know
Instantly I know
That's where they're keeping their stash.
It's not like when we used to go.
It's different rules now.
Leave it in your jeans or coat pocket now and someone's going to snatch it when you're busy sucking dick.
And they're naked, all wearing these long white socks stuffed with stamp bags and pills.
I couldn't get over it.
It was like I'd walked into some retro German porno.

It wasn't doing anything for me.
Turned me off. Totally.

I came home. Put the… [baggie] in the vase.

I didn't have the right sock-attire anyway.

Was wearing his socks, actually.

KYLE *looks down at* JUDE*'s socks.*

Not now.

He laughs.

You won't see Sam in white socks.

God, no. His socks are much worse.

Just sometimes
Feels nice to walk around like that.

Beat.

I joined this network, this / –

KYLE Network?

JUDE Support network,
This…
Group.
Support [group]
For support.
For when people die.

KYLE Right.

JUDE Surprised myself really.
Didn't really have myself down as 'the type'.

KYLE Can't say I saw you as…

Gestures.

…in a 'group'.

JUDE I listen mainly.

It's online.
I keep my camera off and listen.

There's this woman, this dentist, she –
Her husband died and now she's
She's the same.
Horny all the time.
Slept with hundreds of men since.
Maybe not hundreds.

She met this guy from South Africa on a chat thing or whatever.
Flew all the way out there just to fuck him.

I don't know, I just…

All I can think about is sex and I feel terrible about it but I can't stop the craving.

What is that?
Is that like… a *thing*?

Maybe it's wanting to be in the moment, in my body.
Respite, maybe. Is that it?

,

Work didn't have your number.

I gave it to them.

If you go to hospital, they have to call someone.
HR. It's the policy

Jenny asked who.

I said you.

Silence.

KYLE You've got other exes.

JUDE Not really.

KYLE You know other people.

JUDE What people?

KYLE Why didn't you call someone else?

JUDE Didn't think you'd want me at those kinds of parties on my own.

KYLE I don't.

JUDE I can't trust anyone else sober.
Maybe I can.
Maybe I feel too guilty unless I'm spun out.

KYLE I thought I 'abandoned' you.

JUDE You did.

KYLE Now you trust me?

JUDE Before then.
Before everything… blew up.
I trusted you then.

Thought maybe we could
Pretend none of that happened
That none of this…

Takes in the apartment.

(*Re: baggie in the vase.*) Or that.

None of it exists yet.

And just
Be twenty-three again.
Sit in that fantasy.
Some respite, or something.

Silence.

KYLE What you're saying…
What you're asking me, I…

JUDE No, I know, I –

KYLE I'm –
I can't just…

JUDE Let's just
Forget
All that

KYLE Got a flight to catch.
I should probably….

JUDE Yes.

KYLE Get going.

JUDE My throat's quite tight.

KYLE Yeah.
Me too.

JUDE I think I'm about to throw up.
Sorry.

KYLE Oh.
Are you okay?

JUDE Might be the sauce.
Or the wine, or

KYLE Do you want… [help]?

JUDE No no I'm…
Give me a sec.

He walks into the bathroom with surprising decorum.

Silence.

KYLE*'s phone rings.*

A moment.

He takes a deep breath…

and answers.

KYLE Hey, you.
How's –

JUDE *pokes his head out of the bathroom. He stands next to the door, quietly listening.*

KYLE *doesn't see him.*

Babe, babe –

No, don't do that,
That's not sensible, is it?
I'm talking to you now, aren't I?

Can we talk about this at home.
I'm coming home now.

You don't mean that.

I –
About to drive home.

Went to the launch, then for a drink with the Olympia guys

I sent you a text.

Why did you –
Okay.
I think that's a bit…

Well, no, I didn't go, no, which is why my name wasn't ticked off the list –

Yes, I'm fine.
I'll explain when I'm back.
I'm already packed.

Because you worry.
I'd knew you'd get –

What do you mean outside?
What stuff?
My clothes?

Don't say that.

Of course I do. You're being irrational.

Bring it inside then, please.
We'll talk when I'm –

Hello?

Josh?

Are you –

Disconnect tone.

A moment.

He looks at the phone. Then puts it down.

JUDE *disappears back into the bathroom before* KYLE *sees him.*

Silence.

Jude?

JUDE (*Off.*) Yeah.

KYLE You good?

JUDE (*Off.*) It's not following up.

KYLE You'll feel better once it's out.

JUDE (*Off.*) I know
That's why I'm…

Silence.

Eventually, we hear him vomit.

A moment.

KYLE *grabs the bottle and takes a swig.*

JUDE *runs the tap. Gargles. Spits.*

KYLE Okay.

JUDE*'s back.*

Let's do it.

JUDE My eyes are watering.
Are my eyes watering?

KYLE Got to get some stuff
Won't be able to fit it all in the car
I'll bring what I can and the rest I'll

JUDE What stuff?

KYLE Just the irreplaceables.
Laptop, photos, my best jumpers
There's not much
I can leave most of it

JUDE Take it where?

KYLE Here.

JUDE Why are you taking it here?

KYLE Unless you want to find somewhere else?
Move somewhere new
Fresh start.

JUDE Move somewhere new?

KYLE Just a room somewhere until this place sells.

JUDE Together?

KYLE Maybe a two-bed. I work from home.

JUDE That's not what I'm saying.

KYLE What?

JUDE I'm not asking to get back together.

KYLE Why not?

JUDE *laughs.*

JUDE Why not, Kyle?
I don't know
Maybe because you're married to someone else?
Yes, yep, that's it, that'll be the reason.

KYLE It's a bit rocky.

JUDE I figured.

KYLE This is what we both need.
A fresh start.

I know you, Jude.

JUDE You haven't even seen me in years
I definitely don't know *you*.

KYLE Yes you do. It's us. It's the same us.

JUDE You could be anyone.

KYLE I think about you.

When Josh and I…
Sometimes
When we're…

JUDE Kyle –

KYLE I think about you.
About different people.
About fucking you.

JUDE I don't need to know that.

KYLE If I can't come, I think about us sometimes.
Wank over the photos of us
At parties

JUDE Right.

KYLE Sometimes I feel like I've being doing things, I've been going through life doing things just so I could do them again with you. Making memories and banking them, so when you call me up and ask me if I want to watch the sunset, I'll have this archive of hills and benches and viewpoints and where to watch the sun set the best in winter or spring or San Francisco or after an awesome day or after an awful day or when you've been mugged or got a promotion or broken a toe or your mum's brought you more of those charms for that bracelet you never wear or when you're hungry or feeling inspired I'll be able to say… Yes. I know where we should go.

JUDE Why are you telling me this?

KYLE We've never done this
Without parties, without pick-ups.

JUDE Kyle.

KYLE Maybe it would be different this time.
Maybe we should try

JUDE No.

KYLE Sit in the fantasy.
Be twenty-three.
Start over
Like you said

JUDE That's not what I said.

KYLE Do you ever think about the people we could have been if we got to know the people we were and decided to be better than them?

JUDE I don't want to do that.

KYLE We can.

JUDE I'm making a coffee.
Do you want one?

KYLE No, I…
What?
Jude, I'm –

JUDE *starts making coffee.*

JUDE My head's spinning.

KYLE A coffee?

JUDE It's an espresso machine.

KYLE No. No, thank you.

JUDE Someone gave it to me when he died.
Thought it was a bit odd.
'Fuck flowers. Have an espresso machine'

It's the best funeral present I got.

Funny because
Sam fucking hated coffee.

Even iced coffee.
What sort of dysfunctional gay doesn't like iced coffee?

The dead ones, apparently.

He waits for the espresso machine.

,

With us, me and you, I think…

,

The booze and the drugs and the sex and risk taking and the just bringing out the worst versions of each other
It didn't break us.

It sort of *was* us.

,

He wasn't that.

Silence.

KYLE Did you ever…
Whilst we were together
Were you and him ever…

,

Because you knew him.

That party we went to at your new firm. He was there.

JUDE He'd started a few months before me.

KYLE Were you already seeing him?

JUDE We hooked up once.

KYLE ,

Yeah.

,

I think I knew that.

JUDE It wasn't romantic.

We didn't really speak again until…
He was there when I needed someone.

Silence.

KYLE *goes to take the bottle.*

(*Stopping him.*) Hey.

A moment.

KYLE *puts it down.*

Silence.

KYLE He got this dream job.
On the other side of the world.

And I'm…

,

I thought I'd had an epiphany, or something when they called about you.
Isn't that ridiculous.

I think I thought it was some divine fucking intervention, or something.
Driving to some… god-awful book launch, for some illustrator who I probably met at some else's god-awful book launch.

And you called.

And now I'm here and you've got this place, this stunning apartment, really.

It's lovely.

Silence.

JUDE You don't want this.

Gestures. Takes in the apartment.

All this, with me.
You don't.

Whatever it is
Whatever's not working
Whatever job you're not doing that you want to be doing

It's not gonna get fixed here.

We never fixed anything.

They laugh.

I don't need fixing.
I need fucking. And cuddling. And to get some sleep.

JUDE *rubs his eyes*.

KYLE Don't touch / your stitches.

JUDE I'm not, I'm…
Rubbing my eyes.

Tired.

Haven't slept since Sam.

,

Wish you could just buy it, you know.

KYLE Tiredness?

JUDE Like a pill.
Instant rejuvenation.

Just buy it over the counter.
'Yes, I do have a Boots card, thank you.'

Or drink it like a potion.
Or slam it.
I'd even slam it, wouldn't you?
Less painful than lying down with your thoughts.

Silence.

KYLE Okay.
Okay, so…
What do we…?

What's the plan?

JUDE Haven't *planned*, Kyle.
There's no plan.

KYLE What would you like to…
I mean…
That's what I mean.
What would you like to happen?

JUDE I don't know, Kyle.
I don't know what I'm…

Haven't thought about this bit.

KYLE No, okay.

JUDE Sort of thought we just…
We have sex
And go to sleep
And wake up in the morning
And I ring HR and let work know I'm not coming in
And you have a look at the flush because you're pretty sure you can fix it but you can't
And you get angry. That cute, frustrated state you get yourself into
And I tell you it's okay because I can't do it either
And we find a plumber and book him in, and book someone in to fix the washing machine
And we tidy all this up
And eventually you put my coat on, and drive back to Josh and make up some story which you've probably already begun to make up about where you were and what you've done
And you make your flight, and you move to Singapore

And you do some more children's books, take on a side job, and get divorced, or a Cocker Spaniel, or both.
And I stay here
And eventually I stop buying and binning new suits. I don't repaint the walls or rip out the bathrooms. I settle on a wallpaper that doesn't make me want to puke
And go to work
And talk to the fridge
And slowly wear his socks less.

Silence.

KYLE Jude.

JUDE I know.

,

I can't expect you to do that.

Silence.

I'll make up the bed. You can sleep there.
I crash out on the sofa most nights anyway.

KYLE *walks over to* JUDE.

He kisses him.

Hey
We –

They kiss again.

If you're –

KYLE I'm not.

JUDE We can just sleep.
You can see how you feel in the morning.
If you still want to.

KYLE I want to.

,

I want to help.

That's why I'm here, isn't it?

,

Do you still [want to]? –

JUDE *kisses* KYLE.

KYLE *takes his top off.*

Slides down his trousers.

He takes off JUDE*'s hoodie.*

They kiss.

He goes to take off JUDE*'s vest.* JUDE *gently stops his hand. He keeps it on.*

They kiss.

JUDE *slides down his joggers. He's struggling.*

It's okay. I'll –

JUDE Can't get it

KYLE I've

JUDE Trying

KYLE Got it.

KYLE *takes over.*

They kiss.

KYLE *lifts and holds him.* JUDE *wraps his legs round.*

KYLE *carries* JUDE *over to the sofa, lays him on his back.*

JUDE Ahhh.

KYLE Okay?

JUDE Think so.

KYLE Your back?

JUDE I'm fine.

KYLE Sure?

JUDE Cushion.

KYLE *grabs a cushion.*

No, not –

KYLE Which?

JUDE Smaller.

KYLE Here?

JUDE Uh-huh.

KYLE *takes another.*

KYLE Where?

JUDE I'll…

JUDE *takes the cushion from* KYLE. *Positions it so he's comfortable.*

KYLE Better, Goldilocks?

JUDE Just right.

They laugh.

Then they kiss.

Then they laugh.

Then they kiss.

This goes on for a bit.

Until…

JUDE *sits up on the edge of the sofa, facing the wall.*

He's masturbating.

KYLE *waits.*

Getting there.

KYLE Relax.

Silence.

JUDE Are you still hard?

Silence.

Sorry.

KYLE You're not relaxed.

JUDE *stops.*

JUDE Water.
On the left side of the fridge there's a bottle.

KYLE I'll get it.

JUDE Sorry.

KYLE Let's not, you know…
We're not doing all that
Apologising. Let's not.

JUDE Yeah.

KYLE It's us. It's me.
It's happened… how many times?
It's just us.

JUDE Not Sober.
Off our faces, sure.

KYLE Exhausted, you're –
(*Giving him a glass.*) Water.

JUDE Thanks.

He drinks.

They sit together.

Silence.

KYLE If you want to…
If you'll think it'll help…

To pretend I'm him.
If you want to
I don't mind.
If you want to call me…
If you want to use his name.

,

If that helps.

Silence.

JUDE Sometimes it feels like he saved me, and
I couldn't quite save him. You know?

Silence.

Feel like I've just slipped.

I haven't landed on my arse yet but my feet aren't on the floor and I can't ground myself in anything. If you videod someone falling in slow motion. And I'm just here. Mid-slip. Mid-jolt. You know?

Silence.

KYLE*'s fiddling with his moustache.*

KYLE Gonna shave it off.

JUDE Why?
Keep it.
I like.

KYLE I don't know who it is.
It's not me.

JUDE ,

Does *he* like it?

KYLE He does.

JUDE Got good taste.

JUDE *rests his head on* KYLE*'s lap. They cuddle up.*

Silence.

What's one of your stories?

KYLE What?

JUDE Tell me one. Like a *Cute Bedtime Story.*

KYLE Not *my* stories.
I don't write them.

JUDE You illustrate them.

KYLE The illustrations are the best bit.
Everyone knows that.

,

I have started…
You know
Not *writing*, I'm not a [writer] –

JUDE You're writing?

KYLE It's mainly a visual… you know
It's told through –

JUDE Your own story?

KYLE Not published. Not yet.
I don't know.

JUDE Go on.

KYLE I can't really…
It's all illustrations.

JUDE I'll use my imagination.
You used to say I've got a wild imagination.

KYLE You do.

He takes a moment. Thinks of a story to tell.

JUDE *giggles.*

What?

JUDE Start.

KYLE It's a children's story
So…
You know
You're not the target… [audience]

(*Starting.*) One night…

JUDE *puts his thumb in his mouth.*

Yeah okay
I'm not doing this.

JUDE What?

KYLE Sucking your thumb?

JUDE It's my thumb.

KYLE Don't.

JUDE It's a children's story
I'm a child.
Play the game.
You're not playing the game.

KYLE …

JUDE Okay okay I'll stop
Promise.

,

Kyle, I said I promise.

KYLE (*Starting again.*) One night –
You know, it really doesn't work without / the illustrations.

JUDE This is quite stressful. I'm quite stressed.
You've made a children's bedtime story stressful, Kyle.
It's impressive.

KYLE *clears his throat.*

KYLE One night at the beginning of Christmas
A boy wakes –

JUDE So
Christmas Day?
Or…?

KYLE The Christmas Season.

JUDE When's that?

KYLE I don't know
The first of December…?

JUDE You can't just say
The First of December
Like if that's automatically, you know, automatically the beginning of Christmas

KYLE Are you telling the story or am I telling the story?

JUDE Start again.

KYLE Give me a fucking chance.

KYLE *clears his throat.*

It's the *second* of December

JUDE *laughs.*

A boy, the boy in the story, wakes up and looks out of the window. It's snowed overnight. He sees some children in the town on the other side of the valley, he lives on a valley, and they're all sledding down the slope.

Now, his father has bought him this sled, this snow sled.

I'm sort of paraphrasing all this, so…

The boy walks all the way up this big snow-covered hill behind his father's cabin so he can sled down the other side.

When he gets to the top, he notices all these trees growing up the side of the slope.

When starts going down, sledding down the hill, he crashes into one.

Bang.

This big winter spruce.

So he goes all the way up, with this sled. He tries again, and same thing. Crash.

The boy stomps back to his father.

'I can't do it!' he says. 'There are too many trees in the way! Why can't our hill be smooth like the one across the valley?'

His father takes him outside. He points to a small sapling in the ground.

'Pull it out' says the father.

The boy grabs the little tree. He tugs. And he tugs. And pop. Out it comes.

Then his father points to a thorny bush. 'Now try this one' he says.

The boy pulls, but it won't budge.

He tries harder. Finally, out it comes!

Then his father points to a giant pine tree. It stretches all the way up into the sky.

JUDE (*Half asleep.*) What happens?

KYLE The boy wraps his arms around the huge trunk.

He pulls.

And he pulls.

And he pulls.

The tree does not move.

JUDE (*Half asleep.*) No?

KYLE Not one tiny bit.

The father kneels beside the boy.

‘Some things are easy to move. Some things are harder to move. And some things are too deeply rooted to move at all.’

‘But I keep crashing’ says the boy.

The father smiles.

‘You are only looking at the trees’ he says. ‘You are not looking at the spaces in between. The things deeply rooted in the past do not block your path. They shape it.’

So the boy climbs the hill again.

This time he looks carefully.

He doesn’t just see trees.

He sees spaces.

He swerves around one tree
Then another
And another
Faster and faster through the forest he flies
Until he bursts out at the bottom of the hill.

,

He’s done it.

,

And yeah, that’s it, sort of. That’s the story.

Silence.

JUDE*’s fallen asleep.*

That good, huh?

He laughs.

Told you it’s better with pictures.

Carefully, he shifts JUDE*’s head off his lap and onto a cushion. Finds a blanket, places it over him.*

Takes the carbonara pan, empties whatever's left into the bin, then fills it with water from the kitchen tap. Moves toward the bathroom.

JUDE (*Half asleep.*) Where are you?

KYLE Flushing the toilet.

JUDE Later.

KYLE It's on my mind.

JUDE Bucket

KYLE Got the pan.

JUDE [Careful] It's Le Creuset.

KYLE *disappears into the bathroom.*

We hear him flush down the toilet.

KYLE (*Off.*) Flushed.

KYLE *reappears.*

All done.

But JUDE*'s back asleep.*

Silence.

KYLE *collects his clothes from the floor.*

He puts on his trousers. Then his top. Then his jumper.

Picks up Jude's jacket. Thinks about it. Maybe even tries it on. Then hangs it over the back of a chair.

Takes out his phone.

Dials.

It rings for a while. There's no answer. Puts it away.

He moves carefully towards the door. He's trying hard to be quiet.

We hear him opening the door…

…and then, very gently, we hear him close it on his way out.

JUDE *sleeps.*

Below him, the city wakes and moves.

Birds sing.

Cars pass.

The sun rises through the blinds. It fills the apartment.

Eventually, JUDE *turns.*

He sits up slowly. Rubs his eyes.

It's a sunny afternoon now. Maybe the first this year.

He breathes in the new day.

And before he breathes it out again –

End.

IS THIS US FADING OUT

Is This Us Fading Out was first performed at Watford Palace Theatre, on 30 September 2021, with the following cast:

SAMUEL	Jack Harrold
ANTHONY	Miguel Barrulas
Director	Joseph Winer

An earlier version was produced by Swings & Roundabouts, and broadcast live online during the COVID-19 lockdown on 19 July 2020, with the following cast:

SAMUEL	George Fletcher
ANTHONY	Macy Seelochan
Director	Joseph Winer

Characters

SAMUEL
ANTHONY

Note on Text

This play is written to be performed on a bare stage. There should be no scenery, no mime, no props, and no furniture.

(/) indicates the point of interruption in overlapping dialogue.

(…) indicates trailing off.

(–) indicates interruption. Within speech it indicates a break in syntax.

(,) on a separate line indicates deliberate silence from pressure, expectation or desire to speak.

Words in [square brackets] are unspoken, indicating an unfinished thought.

Punctuation is used to indicate delivery, not to conform to the rules of grammar.

One

ANTHONY	Did I?
SAMUEL	Yes. Yes you did.
ANTHONY	Don't remember changing
SAMUEL	It logged me out And now I can't
ANTHONY	That might not be
SAMUEL	Log back in again Because you've changed
ANTHONY	Are you sure you're not typing it wrong?
SAMUEL	I'm sure I'm typing it wrong Because I don't know what I should be typing Because you've changed the password.
ANTHONY	Got so used to the auto-login
SAMUEL	Anthony.
ANTHONY	Yes Okay Fine I changed it I mean Of course I fucking changed it
SAMUEL	Why?
ANTHONY	It's my
SAMUEL	Joint account.
ANTHONY	Account

SAMUEL Knew you'd say that.

ANTHONY Which I pay for

SAMUEL We're paying –
We both paid.

ANTHONY Out of my account.
So, I mean
Technically it's

SAMUEL Right.

ANTHONY My

SAMUEL Yep.

ANTHONY Account.

SAMUEL I get it.

ANTHONY I'm not trying to sound –

SAMUEL Well
You are.
So

ANTHONY I'm not trying to.

SAMUEL You didn't have to…

ANTHONY ?

SAMUEL Straight away.
Change the password.

ANTHONY I don't want to do that.
Keep hold on little bits of our relationship in a Netflix limbo.
We can't do that

SAMUEL I know we can't –
It's not about me and you
You don't have to
Constantly
Treat it like it's about

ANTHONY I haven't

SAMUEL I'm not trying to hop back into bed with you
Believe it or not
I just want to watch some fucking TV
Without you
Patronising

ANTHONY I didn't mean to

SAMUEL I know.
You haven't.
You weren't.
I'm hungry
I'm sorry.

ANTHONY There's –

SAMUEL No
Thank you.

ANTHONY It's left over.
Won't eat it.

SAMUEL I'm fine.

ANTHONY It's just risotto.
Doesn't have to be political.

SAMUEL I didn't know once we broke up I wouldn't have Netflix.

It's all…
Change.

,

I'm happy about it.

Not happy, but

ANTHONY I know.

SAMUEL Don't

ANTHONY What.

SAMUEL Let me –
I can say this.
Okay?
Don't talk and let me talk

ANTHONY Okay.

SAMUEL …

ANTHONY ?

SAMUEL I…
I don't know.

What do I do now?

ANTHONY I don't know.

SAMUEL I've got to set up my own.
Account.

ANTHONY If you want.

SAMUEL I'm behind because of you.

ANTHONY You haven't started –

SAMUEL Still on season three, I know.

ANTHONY It gets shit.

SAMUEL Really?

ANTHONY I stopped watching.

SAMUEL Really!

ANTHONY I only watched it because you watched it.

SAMUEL Oh.
So
You were never that into it
Or?

ANTHONY I don't know.
Maybe not.

SAMUEL It's my favourite show.

ANTHONY I know.
Just not mine.

SAMUEL Got to 'choose a plan'
Look.

ANTHONY Right.

SAMUEL Which one did we…?
Which one do you *still*

ANTHONY Erm

SAMUEL Actually

ANTHONY I don't…

SAMUEL Don't really want to do this now

ANTHONY Standard, I think?

SAMUEL I'll do it later.

ANTHONY Okay.

SAMUEL Okay

ANTHONY Okay.

SAMUEL ,

I'm going to have the risotto.

Two

ANTHONY Wanted to wait.
That's what they say.

SAMUEL Who?

ANTHONY Twenty-one days no contact.
Then after twenty-one days you can reach out.

SAMUEL Who says that?

ANTHONY	Science.
SAMUEL	No one says that.
ANTHONY	Everybody knows the twenty-one-day rule
SAMUEL	So for twenty-one days We weren't allowed to see each other
ANTHONY	Which we did. No contact.
SAMUEL	Except I didn't know that's what we were doing
ANTHONY	Exactly. And I wasn't going to ruin it
SAMUEL	Giving me the / magazine
ANTHONY	Giving you – Exactly.
SAMUEL	Twenty-one days
ANTHONY	Exactly.
SAMUEL	And now you've invited me here to give me my October issue of *Vogue Man*.
ANTHONY	I kept it in this plastic wallet.
SAMUEL	But we're in March.
ANTHONY	Right.
SAMUEL	It's been
ANTHONY	Also, I forgot. That was also –
SAMUEL	Four months
ANTHONY	I'm sorry.
SAMUEL	What about the other months?
ANTHONY	What months?

SAMUEL	The ones between October and March
ANTHONY	Oh. Erm.
SAMUEL	November? December? January?
ANTHONY	I only got the October issue. They just stopped coming after that. I thought you changed the shipping address.
SAMUEL	Yeah to Abi's garage?
ANTHONY	You're living with your sister?
SAMUEL	Thank you for this and… Thanks.
ANTHONY	I can show you how / to change it.
SAMUEL	No. Online? I'll figure it out.

Three

SAMUEL	I'm in Tesco In fact No I'm not. I'm not even *in* Tesco I'm thinking about going to Tesco And suddenly I'm like My blood pressure It shoots right up. Panic. Because if I go to Tesco I might see you You'd be there

In the egg aisle
Checking the eggs
Opening the boxes and checking the eggs and
My throat closes
It really closes
Really
Closes up
And I'm like
Helloooooo I'm trying to breathe please don't do that
But I never bumped into you before in Tesco
Before we met
Even through we've lived in the same place for
How long?
And never once did we –
But now
I'm in Tesco
And I am about to turn into the egg aisle
And I am having this fucking anxiety attack.

And I don't understand because
We ended well.
Really well.
And it was all very amicable and great, and that is great
And this could work for us
Living so close
Because we like each other
Genuinely
As people
Like each other.
But it's been three months
And now this feeling
And maybe we can't
Live in the same place any more
And we need to live further away.

ANTHONY Move?

SAMUEL I've been thinking about it.

ANTHONY You love it here.

SAMUEL I know

ANTHONY It's not that kind of job.

SAMUEL Exactly.

ANTHONY You can't get up and leave.

SAMUEL Not like your job.

ANTHONY Sorry?

SAMUEL You could be anywhere.
I couldn't.
You know that.
I need to be here.
Which isn't the case for you.

ANTHONY ,

Right.

SAMEUL And you're single
So there isn't really reason / you'd need to say.

ANTHONY You think I'm single?

SAMUEL Your Grindr profile is four rows below mine.

ANTHONY You're on… [Grindr]?

SAMUEL If that's not an indication we're way too close, then…

ANTHONY So I've got to move?

SAMUEL Someone's made an offer.
On the flat.

ANTHONY When?

SAMUEL Above asking.

ANTHONY How much above?

SAMUEL Yesterday.
Erm, not much, not…
A few grand.

ANTHONY But it's a buyer's market, that's what they're saying.

SAMUEL Elaine's good.

ANTHONY Said it could take years.

SAMUEL Well, as good as estate agents get
Which is

ANTHONY A few grand?

SAMUEL And that's yours, that's…
Half of it, anyway
Enough to…
If you wanted…
Invest in somewhere new

ANTHONY Right.

SAMUEL Stuff's coming up all the time.
Trowbridge is nice.

ANTHONY Where the fuck is that?

SAMUEL Trendy.

ANTHONY *Trowbridge?*

SAMUEL It's up-and-coming.

ANTHONY Far away.

SAMUEL That's the point.

ANTHONY You've planned this.

SAMEUL I just think

ANTHONY Bet you talked it through with Elaine.

SAMUEL She's doing us a good deal.

ANTHONY Is she?
Well, thank fuck for Elaine.

SAMUEL We can list with someone else.
If you don't want the deal –

ANTHONY What if I don't want to move?

SAMUEL I don't know.

,

Maybe do it anyway.

Four

SAMUEL The contract was only twenty-four months and when that expired the visa expired so now…
I'm here.
Again.

ANTHONY You look really…
Fleshed out.
Good.
Arms.

SAMUEL It's the sun.
The summers are, urgh, chef's kiss, you know.

ANTHONY When I heard you'd left I thought
Basingstoke.
Maybe Woking.
And they said
No, no. He's in Cape Town now
And I was like
Whoa.
Cape Town South Africa Cape Town?

And okay
Maybe for a couple of months, sure, but

SAMUEL Didn't feel long.
Flew by.

ANTHONY Two years is a long time.

SAMUEL ,

This party is…

ANTHONY It's a bit shit, isn't it.

SAMUEL The music is a choice.

ANTHONY Who made the quiche?

SAMUEL She used to flog her home-made moisturiser on Facebook.
Helen.
Do you remember?

ANTHONY Probably tasted better.

,

You didn't say anything.
When you left.
I thought you'd…

SAMUEL Back now, anyway.

ANTHONY Long?

SAMUEL Two weeks

ANTHONY And then?

SAMUEL Helsinki.

ANTHONY Obviously.

SAMUEL The company are expanding.
It means I'm still doing what I'm doing

ANTHONY Sure.

SAMUEL Just not here.

ANTHONY That's good.

SAMUEL Everything fell into place at the right time.

Five

ANTHONY I'm masturbating and thinking about you a lot.

SAMUEL Okay.

ANTHONY A lot.

SAMUEL Right.
I mean
That's nice.

ANTHONY What?

SAMUEL No, no, it's

ANTHONY Don't be a dick.

SAMUEL I'm not.

ANTHONY I'm being vulnerable here.

SAMUEL Really nice
Actually
It feels quite nice to know that

ANTHONY I mean it's just…
Fuck.
You are…
You are 'wow'

SAMUEL I'm standing awkwardly.
I'm not sure how to respond.
Don't stop talking.

ANTHONY Because I knew you.
Like I fucking knew every part

And now
I'm scrolling
And you've got this photo
And you're shirtless fishing in fucking
In the fucking Arctic / fishing

SAMUEL Finland.

ANTHONY And I'm like
Fuck me.
Because I didn't know you
You
That you
You know
Went to…
And now there's this whole person that you are
That you've become since we
Since you and me
Killed us off
Since then
There's this new Samuel
Who's in Finland and looks fit
And this new Samuel on Instagram
The Finland one.
Him.
I haven't fucked him yet
And I really want to.

,

Really

Really
Want.

Six

SAMUEL	Don't
ANTHONY	Fuck Sorry.
SAMUEL	Stop with all the pressure.
ANTHONY	I don't know what's wrong
SAMUEL	I can see inside your head. I can feel it with all the pressure Pressure Pressure
ANTHONY	I'm not normally…
SAMUEL	It makes it worse.
ANTHONY	We've never had this.
SAMUEL	We haven't done *this* in years.
ANTHONY	I don't know what's
SAMUEL	I can google…
ANTHONY	Google?
SAMUEL	Things that might, you know
ANTHONY	No?
SAMUEL	Solutions
ANTHONY	*Solutions?*
ANTHONY	That might help.
ANTHONY	Don't google, don't fucking google, why would you google?
SAMUEL	Create a *mood*, or whatever
ANTHONY	By googling? Stop. Please stop.

SAMUEL Okay.

ANTHONY I'll be fine.
Give me a second.

SAMUEL ,

You can always take…

ANTHONY Hang on.

SAMUEL If you have one.

ANTHONY What?

SAMUEL Little blue pill.

ANTHONY I'm not even thirty.

SAMUEL Age isn't always / –

ANTHONY Sammy.

SAMUEL Sorry.

ANTHONY Please.

SAMUEL Take a breath.

ANTHONY Fuck.
Okay.

,

Sorry.

SAMUEL Close your eyes.

ANTHONY I've tried

SAMUEL Anthony.

ANTHONY Okay.

SAMUEL Because we don't have to do the animal fucking.
We can just touch noses
And kiss each other's thighs
And stroke each other, slowly

Before you get yourself into me
I grip your hair
And we carry on cuddling
And when you're ready
You'll be inside and you'll come
And we touch noses
And kiss each other.

,

How's that?

,

Is that working?

Seven

SAMUEL We should stop.
Maybe.
I don't know.
Yes, I do.

ANTHONY What?

SAMUEL It *is* weird.
After being together and then not being together
And maybe couple of times
Get it out the system
That's healthy.
But seven months of hooking up?
I feel like I'm in purgatory.
We're in some weird sex purgatory.

ANTHONY Sounds hot.

SAMUEL It is hot.
It's just…

Not where I want to be
Any more.

ANTHONY ,

So
Should I go…
Now?

Or have tonight
and then go tomorrow and not come back?

SAMUEL ,

I'll pay for the Uber.

Eight

SAMUEL I'm going back to Finland on Wednesday.

I've met someone.
Just so you don't see it on Instagram or whatever

,

He's nice.

We've been together a while now, actually.

,

I'm thinking about proposing.

Nine

ANTHONY *only.*

Samuel 'is active now'.

ANTHONY Heard about the floods.

Seems pretty bad in Helsinki.

Hope you're okay?

Let me know when you get this message.

…

Samuel 'was last active 1 minute ago'.

Ten

SAMUEL You look…

ANTHONY You too.

SAMUEL You look really
Wow.

ANTHONY Thanks.

SAMUEL A little bit…
Are you?

ANTHONY Huh?

SAMUEL A little drunk.

ANTHONY It's a wedding.
It's part of the Ts and Cs.

SAMUEL You've got a
It's
A little bit of

ANTHONY Not keeping it.

SAMUEL No, no it's…
Keep it.

ANTHONY You think?

SAMUEL Didn't know you could grow a beard.

ANTHONY Me neither.
But
Ta-dah!

SAMUEL He's got a beard.
Helen's new fella.

ANTHONY Husband now.

SAMUEL What do you think?

ANTHONY Cute ceremony, yeah.

SAMUEL ,

Give it a year.

ANTHONY Optimistic.

SAMUEL Year and a half, max.

ANTHONY They look happy.

SAMUEL It isn't for everyone.
Take it from a married man.
Marriage is hard work.

ANTHONY How's that going?

SAMUEL He's here.

ANTHONY I saw.

SAMUEL I'll introduce you.

ANTHONY That's okay.

,

I'm sure he's lovely.

,

Anyway.
Just came over to say hi.
Thought I'd pop over quickly and say hi.
And yeah.

SAMUEL Yeah.
I'm glad you did.

,

Hi.

ANTHONY Hi.

End.

A Nick Hern Book

Slippery and *Is This Us Fading Out* first published in Great Britain in 2026 as a paperback original by Nick Hern Books Limited, The Glasshouse, 49a Goldhawk Road, London W12 8QP

Cover image: John McCrea; photography by Ali Wright; graphic design by William Andrews

Designed and typeset by Nick Hern Books, London
Printed in the UK by Mimeo Ltd, Huntingdon, Cambridgeshire PE29 6XX

A CIP catalogue record for this book is available from the British Library

ISBN 978 1 83904 438 0

Woodland CARBON
www.woodlandcarbon.co.uk
NICK HERN BOOKS
Printed on Carbon Captured paper

www.nickhernbooks.co.uk/environmental-policy

Nick Hern Books' authorised representative in the EU is
Easy Access System Europe – Mustamäe tee 50, 10621 Tallinn, Estonia
email gpsr.requests@easproject.com